FOR THE REAL SACHA

ISBN 978-3-033-05577-3

First edition

Sacha and the witch with no friends

BY
Isaac Cocci

ILLUSTRATIONS BY
MARICZKA RUBAN

SACHA AND THE WITCH
WITH NO FRIENDS

by Isaac Cocci

DAD normally couldn't say no to his son Sacha. Although Dad wanted to go golfing, Sacha insisted that his father drove them to the Cellus-Pit zoo. Dad agreed that Sacha could wear his new red sneakers, even though Dad knew full well they would get dirty. Dad also didn't mind spending hours with the monkeys, Sacha's favorite, although Dad's favorite animal was the lion.

But sometimes Dad had to draw a line. When Sacha heard the bells of the ice cream cart dinging as the vendor came down the path behind them and said, "Dad, I want some ice cream," his father replied, "You just ate breakfast. I'm sorry, but you'll have to wait."

Sacha stopped and pulled on his father's yellow blazer sleeve. "Please, please, *please*, I want ice cream."

"No. Maybe we can move on to see the lions now?"

"I want an ice cream!" the boy insisted.

Mrs. Catwell and her daughter, who were standing in front of the pig's quarters, turned to stare at Sacha and his father. Dad didn't like to draw attention to himself.

He bent down and whispered firmly in Sacha's ear, "No. You just ate and on top of that, last time I gave you ice cream in the zoo, you ate like a pig."

"I beg your pardon?!" The voice came from the pigsty just a few feet away from them. A very big pig stared at Dad. You or I would pinch ourselves at the extraordinary sight of a talking pig. But to the inhabitants of Cellus-Pit, this was quite normal.

Sacha's father, who, as I've said, disliked calling attention to himself, turned away from the pen.

"What do you mean 'ate like a pig'?" the pig said. She swung her rump into the enclosure's fence, making the links rattle noisily. Dad turned back to face her, so he wouldn't appear rude. "Do we have a way of eating that is unpleasant to you?" the pig asked.

"No," Dad said. "I didn't mean to offend you. I just meant that my son got chocolate ice cream all over his shirt last time–"

"Oh, so you think we are messy eaters, do you? Do you see any food on me?"

Sacha and Dad looked at the pig in her sty. The sty was full of mud and poo, but to the pig's credit, there wasn't any food on her.

"You're right. I'm sorry I offended you."

Pig lifted her chin into the air and harrumphed.

"Make sure it doesn't happen again," Pig said.

"Oh, go on! Just buy him the ice cream!" someone shouted from across the walkway.

Sacha and his dad turned their heads. The voice was coming from the monkey park. Sacha's favorite animal was sticking up for him.

As if a talking pig weren't shocking enough, now the monkey was speaking up. You and I would be shocked to witness this.

Dad turned to the monkey. "I beg you to not get involved, Mister Monkey."

"Just buy the ice cream. What do ya gotta lose?" Monkey said.

Sacha choked back a little chuckle.

"Hee hee hee," Monkey laughed. "Loosen up, old chap."

Sacha laughed and looked up at his dad. "Come on, old chap," he said.

Dad's face turned red. "Sacha..." he said in his growly bear voice. Dad put his finger out to shake it at his son, but before he could scold Sacha, someone else spoke.

"Oh, go on, Richard."

Dad froze. He didn't have to turn around because he knew that voice all too well.

Sacha looked behind Dad. "Grandma!" he shouted. She had been dead for four years now. Today she was dressed as nicely as ever. She wore a light yellow blouse and a flowery skirt.

"Hello, my precious," Sacha's grandmother's ghost said. Then she turned to her son. "I used to buy you ice cream all the time. And yes, you got it all over yourself. I just put the clothes in the wash. No big deal."

"Mom, I didn't like you telling me what to do when you were alive." He took Sacha's hand. "Come on. I don't like this zoo anymore. Let's go home."

Dad carried Sacha to the car and they left the zoo – and Sacha's hope for ice cream behind.

A talking pig, a mocking monkey, and the ghost of a grandmother: that was a lot to take in for a first chapter. Maybe the most extraordinary thing was that nobody seemed the least bit shocked by these encounters.

IN Cellus-Pit the extraordinary had replaced the normal. Some days, cats barked and dogs meowed. Trees by the mayor's office grew upside down, reaching to the sky with their roots and planting their treetops in the ground. Every other week, the sun rose in the west and set in the east. Every morning, you rushed to the mirror wondering if your face might be green, blue, or purple. And you thanked goodness if you had your normal skin color.

The people of Cellus-Pit didn't know why these things happened. They just knew it had something to do with the Forbidden Forest. Of course, there were rumors. The elders of the town had warned everyone that a witch was living in the Forbidden Forest and that she was responsible for this strange magic. As is often the case, the elders were not listened to, because they spoke slowly and everybody found them boring. Besides, nobody had seen any sign of a witch for at least fifty or sixty years. Maybe more. Why on earth should anybody believe this story?

Still, parents did not allow children anywhere near the forest. They did not even allow themselves anywhere near the forest. Just because you didn't believe in witches, didn't mean you weren't afraid of witches.

Unfortunately for everyone in Cellus-Pit, and especially for Sacha and his parents, the legend of the witch was true. Right now, only you and I know that the life of our hero, Sacha, was about to change in a dramatic way.

Let me give you some straight facts about the witch. First of all, she hadn't been seen for exactly one hundred years.

She lived in a cottage in the middle of the Forbidden Forest. The witch kept a very fat guard at her door. He was so fat that all he had to do was sit there and block the door with his fat body. He never moved. You may wonder how a man could live such a boring life. He was a very lazy person and was quite content to do nothing but stay in place. The guard was the witch's cousin. She was the only one who could give him a job.

On this day, the witch sat at her dining table, focusing on a book called *The World's Hardest Sudokus: Nobel Prize Edition*. The book contained exactly one hundred sudoku puzzles, and they were so hard that each puzzle took her a year to solve.

There she was, filling in the last numbers on the last page.

"Three. Six. Seven... Finished! Aren't you lucky to have the smartest friend in the world?" the witch said. She looked toward her friends only to find two skeletons sitting on her chairs, with cobwebs between their bones. She got up from her chair and approached the first skeleton. "Wake up," she said, shaking its bones. She looked to the heavens. "What happened? What happened to my friends?"

A little rat leaned against the wall next to his hole. "Your friends are long dead. They were trying to tell you they were hungry, but you were so focused on your sudoku that they starved to death in their chairs."

The witch looked at the rat. "Ebenezus? There's something off about you."

"I'm not Ebenezus," the rat said. "He was my great-great-great-great-grandfather. He's also long dead."

"What are you talking about?" the witch said. "I'm so smart that I did this entire book of puzzles in only five minutes."

"No," the rat said. "It took you a hundred years!"

"Nonsense," the witch said. She rose to her feet, pulled out her wand and cast a spell. The rat fled into his hole. The spell struck the wall, throwing blue sparks every-where.

The witch shook the other skeleton and its skull fell to the floor. "These friends are absolutely useless," the witch said. "I have to go get some new ones."

The rat looked at the chains around the skeletons' arms and legs and said from his hole, "Will you be getting new friends the same way you got these two friends?"

"Ex-friends!" the witch said.

"Will you capture your new friends, too?" the rat asked.

"Yes...err...no! What? Of course not! They are my friends! Shut up or I will change you into an ant."

The rat shut up.

The witch went to her front door. "Out of my way, cousin," she poked his butt with her wand.

The pain made him scream, then he shouted, "I am too big, I cannot move!"

The witch pushed on the guard's back, to no effect. "Grrrrr," she said. She cleared the cobwebs from the window to the right of the door. The witch opened the window and climbed outside. She turned to face her cousin. "Guard the house while I'm away. I'm going out to get some new friends."

SACHA kept his mouth shut until the moment Dad parked the car at their house. "I want to go back to the zoo," Sacha said.

Dad shook his head. "Too much magic there today. Let's stay in our garden. I have a terrific idea. I'll teach you how to ride the bike you got for your birthday. It's been sitting in the garage. "

"I don't want to learn how to bike."

An owl sat on a branch of the birch tree in the garden. "What do you think Owl? Should I learn how to bike if I don't want to?" The owl only blinked. "The animals at the zoo took my side."

The owl shrugged his shoulders. "I don't concern myself with other people's business."

Dad carried the bike outside. He looked at Sacha. "Are you finished?"

The front door of their house swung open. Sacha's Mom stood there, dressed in jeans and a pink polo shirt. Sacha thought she could help him skip the bike lesson.

"What's up, boys?" Mom said.

"Mom, I don't want to learn how to bike."

Mom looked at Sacha. Then looked at her husband. She raised her left eyebrow. This happened when she knew something was going on but couldn't figure it out quite yet.

Sacha said, "Maybe I can hang out with you?"

"It's all because I didn't buy him ice cream," Dad said.

Mom nodded.

"You're going to take me shopping, right, Mom?" Sacha said.

Mom replied, "It's good if you learn how to bike. Most kids your age have learned."

Shock made Sacha's mouth drop. Mom went to Dad and whispered something in his ear. Dad nodded. "Maybe we can strike a deal," she said. "Why don't you learn to bike with your dad? If you make progress, we'll get you ice cream. How about that?"

Sacha nodded. "Ok. Let's do that." He grabbed the handles of his red bike and sat on the saddle. The clean mountain bike tires were ready to travel. He put his two feet on the pedals and immediately lost his balance.

Dad caught the saddle just in time. "Careful!" He held his son up. "Put your feet on the pedals and start pushing." Sacha followed the instructions, as Dad gave him a gentle nudge. But as soon as his father let go, Sacha put his feet on the ground.

"Can't we find a place with some magic, Dad? It would be easier."

"That would be cheating," Dad said. "And you'll get ice cream when you are able to bike all by yourself, not if some magic bikes for you."

Sacha let out a big sigh. He put his feet on the pedals and pushed. Dad ran next to him, holding the saddle. Sacha moved his legs faster and faster.

"You got it," Dad said. "Keep pumping."

Sacha pedaled faster and faster.

"More!" Dad said.

Sacha let out a scream of joy. "Woo hoo! I'm riding a bike! I'm gonna get ice cream!"

Dad let go of the saddle. He couldn't keep up. Sacha biked farther and farther away from his father.

"Dad, how do I stop?"

"Stop moving your legs or hit the brakes!"

But Sacha didn't hear the answer. He rushed away from his dad, afraid of falling off his bike. When he looked back, he couldn't see his house or his parents anymore. He rode through the small town of Cellus-Pit, leaving houses, shops, and cafés behind him. He reached the edge of town and the road he was on turned to gravel and then to dirt. It was leading him right to the Forbidden Forest.

"Sacha!"

Sacha turned back and saw his dad riding a big bike, pumping his legs fast. The first tree of the Forbidden Forest was very close to Sacha now. Dad was still speeding along. Sacha lifted both his feet and leaned to the left. He fell on

the ground and scratched his arm and leg and a bit of his cheek. He had stopped just before entering the Forbidden Forest.

Dad hit the brakes right behind Sacha and kicked up a little gravel. "Quick, come here!" He grabbed his son

and put him over his shoulder. He grabbed the boy's bike
with one hand. His other hand gripped his own handlebars
and he rode away from the forest, breaking a sweat as he
pushed hard. Sacha looked back at the woods. He could
see two little lights between trees. Like a cat's eyes at night.
He shook his head and looked again. The two lights had
disappeared.

YOU have probably guessed that those two little lights were indeed a pair of eyes, and not just any eyes! They belonged to the witch with no friends. When the witch saw Sacha's dad, she said to herself, "Ooh, look at this new friend! What a handsome man!"

She watched him bike away, as he carried Sacha on his shoulder and held a small bike. She said, "He is so strong and so fast!" Her gaze followed him until he reached his home and made a mental note of where he lived.

The witch waited until night fell on Cellus-Pit. Around midnight, the wicked witch with no friends rode her broom to Sacha's house. She peeked through a bedroom window and saw Sacha's parents sleeping.

"Not just one, but two new friends! Even better!" she said to herself. "Don't they look so smart and interesting?" She opened the window and poked her head inside. "They look so peaceful and happy when they sleep. These are exactly the kind of friends I like."

She climbed into the large bedroom and stood on a red rug at the foot of the bed. Mom and Dad had snuggled themselves under a cotton bed sheet.

"I already love them," she said. "You two won't just be my friends. You will be my best friends."

Her voice woke Dad and he opened an eye to discover the face of the witch right in front of him. Have you ever woken up to see a witch's face staring at you from only a few inches away? I haven't, but I can understand why he screamed at the top of his lungs. Mom woke up and she screamed at the top of her lungs, too.

Dad jumped out of bed and raised two fists. The witch took her magic wand out of her pocket and thrust it toward Dad. A green bolt of lightning travelled from the wand to Dad's chest. The spell froze Sacha's father. He couldn't move his arms or legs.

"Easy, easy," the witch said. "Is that how you say hello to your best friend?"

"Who are you and what do you want?" Dad said.

"I've come to pick you up. You'll have a lot of fun at my house in the forest."

Mom kept a book as big as the dictionary on her bed-side table. She grabbed the book, stood up, and smashed it over the witch's head. The witch took a step back and wobbled.

"That hurt," the witch said. "How could you do that to your friend?"

The witch used her wand to cast a spell on Mom. Now, Mom was frozen, too.

"Let us go, you evil woman!" Dad said.

But the witch took Mom, carried her out the window and tied her with a rope on the broom the witch had left outside. She did the same with Dad. Both parents screamed "Help!" They hoped to wake the neighbors. "Aren't we having fun, all of us, together?" the witch said. She sat on her broom and flew back to her forest.

Sacha was a deep sleeper. He didn't hear any of this happening.

THE sun streamed in Sacha's bedroom window. He woke up to the usual sights: his gray teddy bear and his ceiling decorated with stars, but he couldn't smell bacon and toast. Nor could he hear the sound of his mother clanging pans as she prepared oatmeal and eggs. "Mom!? Dad!?" He waited in bed. Normally his parents rushed to his room if he called out.

Nobody came. He shouted their names again, but only silence answered.

"Have my parents gone deaf?" he wondered. He stood up and walked to the hallway. He called again. He waited for a reply. Nothing. He walked to his parents' bedroom. Only the bed, two bedside tables, and a wardrobe stood in the room. No sign of Mom and Dad.

He searched the entire house, in every room, behind every door, even under every piece of furniture. He could not find them. He sat on the carpet in the living room and started to cry.

What was he going to do? Who would take him to school? Who would give him a hug? The empty house didn't have any answer.

WE have all learned that if we lose sight of our parents, we should stay where we are until they come back.

Obviously, whoever made that rule didn't think of parents being kidnapped by witches. I wouldn't dare to think what would have happened if Sacha had just stayed in his living room. Don't worry, though, he quickly decided to find help in the only place he knew where to find it: the zoo. Hadn't the animals stuck up for him the day before? They would surely help him today.

Before leaving, he went to the kitchen, climbed on a stool, and opened a high cupboard to take a brownie Mom had made the day before. He put it in his pocket, thinking he would need it later. He called for Mom and Dad one last time. Silence met him again, so he went outside. Tears intermittently rolled down his cheeks.

He spotted his small red bike leaning against the garage door. Since he had learned how to bike, he picked it up, sat on it, and decided to pedal in the direction of the zoo. He biked through the gate of the zoo and to the jungle park. Monkey, his favorite animal, lived there. The monkey saw the little boy crying and said, "What's going on, Sacha?"

"I've lost my parents," the boy said. "I woke up this morning and they were gone."

"They can't be gone," Monkey said.

"I waited for hours, but no one came. They didn't warn me. Dad was upset with me yesterday. Do you think they've had it with me?"

"No, never in a million years. Wait here." Monkey said, and he dashed out to the woods in the zoo. After a couple of minutes, he came back with two animals that were much bigger and taller than Sacha: Hippo and Giraffe.

"I can't believe what Monkey just told me," Hippo said.

"It's true. My parents are gone," Sacha said.

"What did you do?" Giraffe asked.

Sacha stretched his neck to look up at Giraffe's head in the sky. The boy shrugged his shoulders. "I don't know."

"Parents don't just disappear like that. Maybe they went out shopping. You should wait at home until they come back," Giraffe said.

"I waited three hours already! They wouldn't be away that long," Sacha said.

"Probably not." The giraffe lowered her head to look Sacha in the eye. "They probably left for good or something terrible happened to them."

Sacha couldn't hold back his tears. The monkey said, "Giraffe!"

"What? Isn't it better that he hears the whole truth?" Giraffe said.

"You don't even know what the truth is!" Monkey said.

"Well, it can't be too positive, can it?"

"Move away!" Monkey said, trying to push the big

animal to the side, without success. "Little man, what do your parents normally do?"

"They take care of me!"

"Obviously not now," Giraffe said.

"Shh," Monkey said. "Yes, yes, they take care of you. But when they're not taking care of you, what do they do?"

"I don't know," the boy said. "I've never been there when they weren't taking care of me."

"Ok, but try to think about what they like to do."

Sacha put his hands to his head. This is how he had seen people concentrate. "I can't."

"You gotta think," Giraffe said, "how do you expect us to give you some advice, if you don't have a bit of a think?"

Sacha took a few steps back and sat down.

"What are you doing?" Giraffe said.

"I'm trying to think," the boy said.

"Not like that," Monkey said. "You gotta think on your feet."

"Why?"

"Because thinking on your feet is the only thing that will get you out of situations."

Sacha stood up. He didn't say anything for two minutes. The hippo said, "What's he doing?"

"I don't know," Monkey said.

"Well, I'm on my feet," Sacha said.

"It's not good enough to be on your feet you gotta think on your feet" Giraffe said.

The monkey laughed and Sacha cried because he didn't like to be mocked. "But how do you think?" the boy said. "I don't know how."

"You just think!" Giraffe said. "How do you look for your parents? You try to find someone who may have information to help you. It's really not that complicated."

"Easy, Giraffe," Monkey said. "Maybe he's a bit young to think on his own. Did your parents teach you to think?"

"Not really," the boy said, "because they usually do all the thinking for me. I just have fun... they do the thinking."

"And you should!" Hippo said. "Children should enjoy life. Parents can do the thinking."

"Well, you see what happens when the parents leave," Giraffe said, "the boy can't even think on his own! We gotta do it all for him."

"Who can I ask about my parents?" Sacha said.

The giraffe turned her back on the boy. "I've had enough."

The monkey approached Sacha. "Don't mind her, she's all high and mighty."

"She always likes to think at a higher level," Hippo added.

"She always says, 'Let's take a giraffe's-eye view,'" Monkey said.

They laughed but Sacha didn't understand why. He wasn't in the mood to laugh anyway. He remembered his parents and tears rolled down his cheeks again. "What if they hate me and wanted to leave me behind?"

"You can't think that!" Monkey said.

"The giraffe told me I have to think, so that's what I think."

"Well, if that's what you think, you'd better not think for a while. You seem to be a wonderful boy, and there is no reason why your parents would do that to you," Monkey said.

"Look, Giraffe is annoyed with me because I can't think. Maybe my parents got annoyed too because I can't think," Sacha said.

"Well, there is one person who would know for sure," Monkey said. "The whale."

"Are you crazy?" Hippo said.

Sacha jumped in. "What? Where is the whale? In this zoo?"

"Don't tell him," Giraffe said. "You know this is not a good idea."

"Come on, tell me! I want to see my parents again!"

Monkey approached Sacha. "You humans don't know she exists because she hates humans, and she usually stays away from all of you. She's living in the lake next to the Forbidden Forest."

Sacha said, "I'm sure she'll be fine with me."

"It's not about you in particular," Giraffe said. "She hates humans so much that if she sees you, she will try to eat you."

"That cannot be. I've never harmed anyone. Nobody is mad at me." He grabbed Monkey's arm and begged "Come on, take me to the whale, please! If she's the only one who knows, I want to talk to her."

"Whale is very dangerous," Monkey said. "Are you sure you want to go?"

Sacha nodded.

"You're crazy," Giraffe shook her head way up high on her long neck.

SACHA biked to the lake and Monkey ran beside him. When they got there, Sacha said, "It's hard to believe a whale lives in this lake." The glassy surface spread out for miles.

The monkey walked to the shore and shouted. "Ooh ooh ooh hee hee hee. Come to me, Whale! I need to talk to you."

The still surface of the water broke. A huge bump swelled in front of their eyes. A giant whale, at least one hundred times the size of Sacha, swam to the shore. The boy's jaw dropped.

"Hello my monkey friend," said Whale. "It's always a pleasure to see you."

Water from her blowhole spewed high into the air. Then she spotted the little boy. "What? You have made me come out in the presence of a human?" Whale growled. She bared her teeth. "I will never forgive you." Her tail hit the water. A giant wave sprang out of the lake. Sacha's eyes opened wide. He ran but managed only a couple of steps before the wave crashed onto shore. It drowned both him and the monkey. Sacha swam up to the surface, as he had learned in swimming lessons with Dad. It was harder than at the pool because a current pulled him down.

Monkey hadn't had swimming lessons. He jerked his arms in every direction. He couldn't manage to keep his head above water. Monkey disappeared under the surface. Sacha dove. He had learned to open his eyes underwater and he spotted the monkey. He grabbed the animal's hand and swam back to the surface using one arm. He got close to a tree, grabbed a branch, and held on tight. The wave eventually went back into the lake, leaving Sacha swinging from the tree with one hand, holding his animal companion with the other.

Monkey coughed and shook his head. "I'll take over from here." He grabbed a branch, pulled himself up, then lifted Sacha and sat him on a branch. Monkey looked down at the whale and said, "I can see that you make the biggest beautiful waves in the universe."

Sacha whispered in Monkey's ear, "How can you say that the wave was beautiful when she just tried to kill us?"

Monkey lifted a finger to his mouth, signaling the boy to be quiet. "I'm not surprised, with such a powerful tail, that you make such impressive waves," Monkey said to Whale.

"She wasn't showing us anything beautiful – she tried to kill us," Sacha said. "Even I figured that out! Looks like I can think better than you after all."

"Shhhh," Monkey said. "You're gonna ruin every-thing." He addressed the whale again. "You must be quite a young whale, to splash water in such a splendid way."

Sacha whispered, "You're crazy. That whale obviously looks like she is three hundred years old."

"Really? You think so?" Whale said.

"Absolutely," Monkey answered. "What a fine demonstration of youth and vitality in that wave you made. I'm absolutely amazed."

"Oh, stop it, Monkey! You don't really think so," Whale said.

"Of course I do, I mean every word of it."

And then, Whale blushed. "Oh, will you come and give me a kiss, Monkey?"

"Really? I would love that," Monkey said.

The Whale approached the shore and pushed out her lips.

"Before I do, you have to help my human friend who lost his parents," Monkey said.

"Is his name Sacha?"

"How did you know?"

"The human's parents are with the witch who lives in the Forbidden Forest," the whale said. "I saw them flying last night on her magic broom. When they flew over my lake, I heard the witch say, 'You don't have to worry about your son, Sacha.'"

"What were they doing with the witch?" Monkey said.

"I don't know. They flew too fast for me to hear."

"Can you tell us more?" Monkey said.

"I told you everything I know. Now come and give me a kiss."

Then Monkey grabbed Sacha by the hand and said, "Quick, let's run away!"

Sacha dashed down the tree with the monkey.

Whale, realizing she wasn't going to get a kiss, screamed, "You took me for a fool!" And she raised her tail high in the sky and hit the water again.

Sacha and the monkey landed on the ground with a thud and ran away from the lake. He struggled to catch his breath and with the little bit of air he had in his lungs, he shouted, "I can't run much longer!"

"Come on, Sacha! A little more!" Monkey replied.

The boy ran with all his might, until he tripped on a rock and fell to the ground. He took a deep breath because he expected to be swimming at any moment. The wave reached his feet. Then his ankles. Then his legs... and waist.

But it stopped there. Sacha turned back and watched the wave fade away.

"That was close!" Sacha said as he recovered his breath. "How come she told us where my parents are after you said some nice things?"

"I figured that somebody as old and angry as she is must like flattery. So I told her things she wanted to hear."

"I wish I could have thought of that," Sacha said.

"In time, you will do your own clever thinking," Monkey said.

As they walked away from the lake, they saw in the distance the beginning of the Forbidden Forest, where the witch with no friends held Sacha's parents prisoner.

AS Sacha and Monkey stood in front of the Forbidden Forest, Sacha recognized the place where he fell off his bike. The trees stood tall. Their large black trunks discouraged anyone from entering. Sacha took a step toward the threshold of the Forest.

"What are you doing?" Monkey said.

"I'm going to get my parents."

"No. We have to find a way around the forest."

"The witch lives in the middle of the Forbidden Forest! So why would we go around it?" Sacha said.

The boy took another step and his toes met a black tree root. Cold air enveloped Sacha's body.

"Yes, we can go above it," Monkey said. "I will ask Owl to fly us straight to the witch's house."

Sacha didn't answer. He kept his foot forward and looked deep into the heart of the forest. It was as if all the things around him stopped existing.

"That way we'll avoid going through these trees," Monkey said. "I don't know what you think, but this forest looks quite evil. Are you ok with the plan?"

A thought came into Sacha's head: *Of course I am ok with the plan*. There was something strange about that thought. It felt different than the usual thoughts in Sacha's head.

"Yes, I am ok," Sacha said.

"Great. Stay here, don't walk a step farther. I will get Owl."

Sacha nodded and Monkey turned around and ran, using his arms and legs, which he did when he wanted to run fast. Sacha kept looking at the forest.

My parents are not safe.

Another of these strange thoughts went through his head. It was almost as if it had a different voice.

"I can't just stand here and wait," he said out loud.

And I'm not sure that the monkey knows anything anyway. Is he even coming back?

Sacha checked to see no one was in sight. He took a step into the forest, then another. And then another.

He stayed alert, expecting the trees to do something horrible to him. What if they used their roots and branches to snatch him? The trees, although eerie, left him alone like trees outside of the Forbidden Forest. They stayed rooted in the ground and only moved when the wind blew them. Sacha picked up the pace, determined to find where the witch was keeping his parents.

But as he walked deeper and deeper into a place he couldn't see the edge of, other very dark thoughts came to his mind.

You'll never make it.
The witch will eat you.
You're too small to make it.
You'll never see your parents again.
He wondered what those thoughts were.
Thoughts? You can't have them because you can't think anyway!
He stopped and sat down. Only trees surrounded him. The weight of loneliness tugged at his heart and mind. Nobody could help him deal with these thoughts. Tears rolled down his cheeks.

That's when a little rat scurried out of the woods and said to him, "Little man, the evil trees are putting bad thoughts into your head. Stand up fast and follow me, or it will get worse."

Sacha stood up and followed the rat, but the thoughts kept coming.

This rat is a liar, he made up this story and he wants to harm you. Grab this big rock and knock him on the head.

Sacha grabbed the rock and lifted it behind the rat's back. He stopped himself from throwing it at the animal's neck. Sacha cried again. The rat turned around and saw the rock in the boy's hands.

"What is the problem?" Rat said.

"Leave me here," Sacha said. "I almost hit you with this rock. I am so sorry. I don't deserve your help. I am such an evil boy."

"It's the dark thoughts," Rat said. "You didn't harm me, because you are good inside. You listened to your heart rather than your head. Quick, we are almost out. Follow me."

Sacha followed him and ignored the thoughts in his head.

Why do you follow him anyway? Your parents have abandoned you 'cause they don't like you.

After a couple of minutes Sacha and Rat came to a big clearing. All the bad thoughts disappeared.

"How can you survive in this evil forest?" Sacha said to Rat.

"Because I only have a little brain! The dark thoughts can't get to me."

"What is the use of thinking," Sacha said, "if this is what it's gonna do to me? I wish I had no brain at all."

Owl and Monkey swooped into the clearing. The monkey was holding onto the bird's legs. They landed next to Sacha and Rat.

"I can't believe you didn't listen to me," Monkey said.

"I should have," Sacha said. "I nearly didn't make it. I'm ok now thanks to Rat. We need to move on."

Sacha studied the witch's house in the middle of the clearing.

"I hope you don't plan to go in there," Rat said.

"Yes, I do. My parents are in that house."

"Oh," Rat said. "If I were you, I would just forget about them. The house is guarded by a giant who can crush you with one hand. And even if you manage to pass him, the witch will cast a spell on you. The only way to escape her is through a little hole that only I can fit through."

"Maybe Owl can fly us in?" Sacha said.

"I'm afraid there is no way in from the top," The Rat said. "I know this house inside out."

"I still wanna go," Sacha said.

"Be careful," Rat said. "She is very powerful and has a lot of magic tricks."

"I'll stay with you," Monkey said. Sacha smiled at the monkey to thank him for being such a good friend. Sacha looked at the witch's house and the terrifying giant guarding the door.

"Let's go," Sacha said.

Owl and Rat stayed in the clearing and watched Sacha and Monkey leave to their uncertain fate.

IF you were in front of a monster that was ten times your size, wouldn't fear paralyze you, like a deer in the headlights? I cannot imagine how Sacha was able to do what he did next.

The giant in front of the house was fast asleep. His big belly blocked the house's entrance. It didn't leave an inch of space to get through.

Sacha and the monkey hid behind a bush and considered the giant. His big arm muscles and hands really impressed Sacha. If the giant woke up and spotted them, he could crush them in a second! The boy and the animal looked at each other.

"I'm trying to think," Monkey said. "But I can't think of anything."

"If only we had some tools, we could drill a hole."

Sacha put his hands in his pockets and felt the brownie he had taken from the kitchen as he left the house. He had forgotten all about it. A brownie won't help.... Wait a minute!

His eyes lit up.

"What?" Monkey asked.

"If the guard is so big, he must love food. We're going to lure him out with a chocolate brownie."

"That's brilliant!" Monkey said. "Now I wish I had thought of that."

Sacha proudly held his head up and even swaggered a bit. Then he tiptoed in the direction of the guard and stopped a few feet away from him. Sacha took the brownie out of his pocket and put it on the ground. The guard's nose twitched. Sniff, sniff.

Sacha's blood froze. The giant was waking up! Quickly, the boy and Monkey ran toward a bush next to the gate.

"Hmm, what is this I smell?" The guard awoke. "A chocolate brownie!" The eyes of the guard tripled in size. "I love brownies!" He looked left and right. Sacha and Monkey hid motionless in the bush.

"No one around," the guard said. "That's weird." The guard waited for a moment, then he prepared to stand. He took a deep breath and placed his hands next to his thighs. The weight of the hands shook the ground and a few bats fell off a tree. He pushed himself upright. His face turned red. His arms trembled. He moved a knee and let out a scream of pain. The guard took a few steps toward the brownie. The ground shook so much that a couple of bricks fell from the gate. He bent down to pick up the brownie.

"Let's go," Monkey said.

Sacha rushed toward the door, followed by Monkey. Sacha stepped on a dead branch, snapping it in two. "Craaack!" There was no way the giant missed that.

Without even checking, the boy and the monkey jumped back into the bush.

The guard turned around. "What was that? It came from that bush." He walked toward the hideaway. Sweat ran down Sacha's forehead. What was the giant going to do with them when he found them? Sacha thought everything was lost.

Monkey turned to him, "Good luck, Sacha. You must continue without me."

Before Sacha could say anything, the Monkey stepped out of the bush, jumping and screaming in front of the giant. Over and over, the guard tried to catch Monkey but the animal jumped out of his way each time the giant hands tried to clutch him.

Sacha jumped through the door and dived to the side. He peeked outside to check on Monkey. The giant was out of breath after ten steps of "running" behind the little animal. He stopped and let Monkey escape. Sacha hid in the shadows and waited until the guard put himself back in the door. Sacha surveyed the witch's house. He took a deep breath. He was alone now. He was going to have to rescue his parents without anyone's help.

SACHA stood in the large entrance of the house. In front of him, a blue carpet extended to the other side of the room and led to two open doors. A staircase climbed from the door on the left to an upper floor. From the right door came a light that changed color: orange, blue, red... The boy tiptoed toward the doors. He looked into the room on the right. Large pans simmered on a big stove. Fumes crept out of the pots. A pedestal held up a magic book. Sacha approached it and read the page on display: "Erasing somebody's memory."

Shelves to the right of the stove held little sacks and jars that contained powders of different colors. Stickers explained their content: "Powder of Craziness." "Powder of Happiness." "Powder of Anger." Sacha's eyes stopped at "Powder of Courage." He snatched it. If the rat was telling the truth, Sacha thought, I'm going to need some courage to get my parents back.

He left the cabinet and ascended the steps behind the left door. As he climbed he could hear people talking. He recognized two very familiar voices. They belonged to his father and mother. He also heard the voice of an old lady.

When he reached the top of the staircase, Sacha poked his head out and discovered a big living room. In the middle of the room, his parents sat on a dirty, old brown couch. A low rectangular coffee table in front of the couch and held the book *How to Win Friends and Influence People*. A most horrible lady, with dirty hair and yellow teeth, sat in a worn-out red armchair.

She was the witch with no friends.

"So, what is your favorite movie?" the old witch said.

"I don't know," Mom responded. "I have so many, I can't think of one right now."

"Please try," Dad said. Sacha had never seen him looking so nervous. Sweat ran down his forehead. "Our new..." Dad swallowed hard, "friend would like to know your favorite movie."

What is going on? Sacha thought. Is this why Mom and Dad went away? To discuss their favorite movies with this horrible person?

Suddenly Mom burst into tears. Dad reached out to hold her against him.

The witch stood up. "What is the problem?"

"I can't," Mom said. "Why are you keeping us here? If you want us to be your true friends, then let us go. We need to take care of our little boy, Sacha. He's on his own and probably very afraid."

The witch's face flushed. "I am tired of this Sacha you keep talking about. You should pay attention to your friend, rather than bring other people into the conversation."

"But he is our son," Dad said. "And he needs us."

"I don't care! If I let you go, I know you will never come back."

She clenched her fists and kicked the coffee table. The book flew right at Sacha. He ducked and the book hit the wall behind his head. He hoped the witch didn't see him. The witch stood up. "I'm gonna make some more tea now."

Sacha noticed that chains held his parents prisoner to the couch. The witch walked toward the staircase. Sacha crawled back a few steps and when he was out of sight, he ran down the stairs.

The witch's anger prevented her from hearing the noise coming from Sacha's steps.

"Stupid Sacha," she said. "I don't know who he is, but if I see him, I'll take care of him."

Sacha guessed from the tone of her voice that "take care of him" wasn't something he would enjoy.

At this point, I would have left without further ado, bid the witch's place good-bye and started my own life without my parents.

Sacha hid behind the door at the bottom of the stairs and heard the witch's footsteps go to the other room on the right. The clang of pans reached his ears.

"Darn these fools," the witch said. "I treat them like the best of friends and all they can think about is their little son, Sacha."

These words, despite the tragedy of the situation, couldn't help but delight Sacha's heart.

"I'll make them forget their son! They are my friends!" she said.

Sacha held his breath. He remembered what he read on the magic book earlier: "Erasing somebody's memory." Was the witch planning on making them drink a potion so that they would forget him? Was she so afraid of losing friends that she had to erase Sacha from his parents' memory? Hopelessness overtook him. Think, think! he told himself. How can I save my parents before she erases me from their memory? He came out from behind the door and ran back up the stairs while the witch still had her back turned.

WHEN he reached the living room, Sacha ran to his parents. "Dad! Mom!"

"Sacha!" Dad said.

"My baby." Mom held him in her arms. "This is a dangerous place, you shouldn't have come here."

"I'm here to save you," he said.

Dad said, "Quick, grab her keys!" He pointed at a wooden dining table, where a ring that held at least fifty keys lay out of reach of the chained parents. The boy ran to snatch the keys and gave them to Dad. Dad chose one and tried to insert it in his lock, but it didn't fit. So he tried with the next one, and the next one.

"Once you are free," Sacha said, "we'll hide behind the door and will knock the witch out."

Dad tried another five keys, but none worked. Sacha heard the witch coming up the staircase.

"Quick, Dad! She's coming back!" Sacha said.

Dad wiggled the keys, trying them in the lock but none of them managed to open their shackles. The witch appeared at the top of the stairs holding a tray filled with teacups. She spotted Sacha in the middle of the living room – and the keys in Dad's hands.

"What? Who are you?" the witch screamed. "Are you trying to take my friends away? These friends are mine! You can't steal them away from me. They are the only two friends I've got." She put down her tray and took her magic wand out of her pocket.

Mom screamed, "Don't hurt him!"

You know the witch never granted requests. The boy closed his eyes and thought all was lost. The witch was going to capture him, and that would be the end of it.

"I can't afford to lose these friends again," the witch said.

Sacha wondered why this witch was so afraid of losing her friends. If only she could stop being afraid, she would not hold people prisoner. Then he remembered that his pocket held the Powder of Courage. If he threw the powder at her, she would overcome her fear! And she would work on making true friends! That's great thinking, he told himself.

The witch raised her magic wand in the air. Sacha took the Powder of Courage out of his pocket. He opened the flask and ran toward the witch. Mom screamed, "Sacha!"

The boy jumped in the air. The witch waved her wand and threw a red bolt of lightening at the boy. Sacha threw the powder at the witch. The red spell hit him on the chest and he fell to the floor. Everything went black.

SACHA didn't move an inch and he didn't breathe. Mom and Dad pulled hard on their chains. The powder drifted through the air and landed on the witch's head. She smiled because of what she had done to Sacha.

She walked back to the door and lifted the tray with the tea that would make Mom and Dad forget all about Sacha. She looked forward to being best friends forever with them. Then a thought came to her: Is this really how I want to make friends? That thought really surprised her. She had never thought of it this way. Shouldn't my friends want to be with me, rather than just be chained to me? Another improbable thought. She paid attention to Mom crying.

"What have you done to Sacha? My poor little boy," Mom said.

And the witch thought, Oh, no, what have I done to my friends? I've made them so sad.

Then she said something she never ever thought she would say. "I am so sorry. Let me make it up to you." She raised her wand and cast a golden spell on Sacha's head. The boy woke up and jumped to his feet.

"Yeah, it worked!" he shouted.

The witch cried. She felt ashamed. She grabbed her keys and unchained Mom and Dad.

Then Dad jumped to his feet and grabbed the witch by the collar. "You crazy witch! You will pay for this."

Sacha lifted his hand and said, "No, Dad. Stop." He walked to the witch and held her hand. "She is different now. She has the courage to make real friends."

The witch looked at him and thought that maybe she had made her first real friend. He must be a great friend to be so forgiving. She lent her magic broom to Sacha, Mom, and Dad, and they were able to fly home.

Cellus-Pit heard about what happened. The inhabitants wondered if the witch really had changed like Sacha claimed. When they looked at the forest from the outside, the trees of the forest were a lighter green than before. A city employee ventured into the forest and came back with the witch. The mayor himself stepped forward and said, "Welcome to the community."

You will agree that we couldn't have hoped for a better ending. Sometimes, the witch came to Sacha's home for tea on Sundays. Rat accompanied her, as he had become a real friend to her. Sacha and his family also had a visit from Monkey. Giraffe and Hippo stayed out in the garden because their size prevented them from entering the house. However, Sacha never heard of Whale again, because not everybody changes.

THE END

Visit
www.isaaccocci.com

Follow
@isaaccocci
For more information about Isaac Cocci's books